Four Letters From Sir Isaac Newton To Doctor Bentley Containing Some Arguments In Proof Of A Deity

Isaac Newton

FOUR
LETTERS

FROM

Sir Isaac Newton

TO

Doctor Bentley.

CONTAINING

Some ARGUMENTS

IN

Proof of a DEITY.

LONDON:

Printed for R. and J. DODSLEY, *Pall-Mall,*
M DCC LVI.

LETTERS, &c.

LETTER I.

To the Reverend Dr. RICHARD BENTLEY, *at the Bishop of* Worcester's *House in* Park-street, Westminster.

SIR,

WHEN I wrote my Treatise about our System, I had an Eye upon such Principles as might work with considering Men, for the Belief of a Deity, and nothing can rejoice me more than to find it useful for that Purpose. But if I

B   have

have done the Public any Service this way, it is due to nothing but Industry and patient Thought.

As to your first Query, it seems to me that if the Matter of our Sun and Planets, and all the Matter of the Universe, were evenly scattered throughout all the Heavens, and every Particle had an innate Gravity towards all the rest, and the whole Space, throughout which this Matter was scattered, was but finite; the Matter on the outside of this Space would by its Gravity tend towards all the Matter on the inside, and by consequence fall down into the middle of the whole Space, and there compose one great spherical Mass. But if the Matter was evenly disposed throughout an infinite Space, it could never convene into one Mass, but some of it would convene into one Mass and some into another, so as to make an infinite Number of great Masses, scattered at great Distances from one to another through-

throughout all that infinite Space. And thus might the Sun and fixt Stars be formed, fuppofing the Matter were of a lucid Nature. But how the Matter fhould divide itfelf into two forts, and that Part of it, which is fit to compofe a fhining Body, fhould fall down into one Mafs and make a Sun, and the reft, which is fit to compofe an opaque Body, fhould coalefce; not into one great Body, like the fhining Matter, but into many little ones; or if the Sun at firft were an opaque Body like the Planets, or the Planets lucid Bodies like the Sun, how he alone fhould be changed into a fhining Body, whilft all they continue opaque, or all they be changed into opaque ones, whilft he remains unchanged, I do not think explicable by meer natural Caufes, but am forced to afcribe it to the Counfel and Contrivance of a voluntary Agent.

The fame Power, whether natural or fupernatural, which placed the Sun in

B 2 the

the Center of the fix primary Planets, placed *Saturn* in the Center of the Orbs of his five fecondary Planets, and *Jupiter* in the Center of his four fecondary Planets, and the Earth in the Center of the Moon's Orb; and therefore had this Caufe been a blind one, without Contrivance or Defign, the Sun would have been a Body of the fame kind with *Saturn, Jupiter*, and the Earth, that is, without Light and Heat. Why there is one Body in our Syftem qualified to give Light and Heat to all the reft, I know no Reafon, but becaufe the Author of the Syftem thought it convenient; and why there is but one Body of this kind I know no Reafon, but becaufe one was fufficient to warm and enlighten all the reft. For the *Cartefian* Hypothefis of Suns lofing their Light, and then turning into Comets, and Comets into Planets, can have no Place in my Syftem, and is plainly erroneous; becaufe it is certain that as often as they appear to us, they defcend into the Syftem

of

of our Planets, lower than the Orb of *Jupiter*, and sometimes lower than the Orbs of *Venus* and *Mercury*, and yet never stay here, but always return from the Sun with the same Degrees of Motion by which they approached him.

To your second Query, I answer, that the Motions which the Planets now have could not spring from any natural Cause alone, but were impressed by an intelligent Agent. For since Comets descend into the Region of our Planets, and here move all manner of ways, going sometimes the same way with the Planets, sometimes the contrary way, and sometimes in crofs ways, in Planes inclined to the Plane of the Ecliptick, and at all kinds of Angles, 'tis plain that there is no natural Cause which could determine all the Planets, both primary and secondary, to move the same way and in the same Plane, without any confiderable Variation: This must have been the Effect

fect of Counfel. Nor is there any natural
Caufe which could give the Planets thofe
juft Degrees of Velocity, in Proportion
to their Diftances from the Sun, and other
central Bodies, which were requifite to
make them move in fuch concentrick
Orbs about thofe Bodies. Had the Planets
been as fwift as Comets, in Proportion to
their Diftances from the Sun (as they
would have been, had their Motion been
caufed by their Gravity, whereby the
Matter, at the firft Formation of the
Planets, might fall from the remoteft Re-
gions towards the Sun) they would not
move in concentrick Orbs, but in fuch
eccentrick ones as the Comets move in.
Were all the Planets as fwift as *Mercury*,
or as flow as *Saturn* or his Satellites; or
were their feveral Velocities otherwife
much greater or lefs than they are, as
they might have been had they arofe from
any other Caufe than their Gravities; or
had the Diftances from the Centers a-
bout which they move, been greater or

lefs

less than they are with the same Velocities; or had the Quantity of Matter in
the Sun, or in *Saturn, Jupiter,* and the
Earth, and by consequence their gravitating Power been greater or less than it is;
the primary Planets could not have re-
volved about the Sun, nor the secondary
ones about *Saturn, Jupiter,* and the Earth,
in concentrick Circles as they do, but
would have moved in Hyperbolas, or
Parabolas, or in Ellipses very eccentrick.
To make this System therefore, with
all its Motions, required a Cause which
understood, and compared together, the
Quantities of Matter in the several Bodies of the Sun and Planets, and the
gravitating Powers resulting from thence;
the several Distances of the primary
Planets from the Sun, and of the secondary ones from *Saturn, Jupiter,* and
the Earth; and the Velocities with which
these Planets could revolve about those
Quantities of Matter in the central Bodies; and to compare and adjust all these

Things

Things together, in so great a Variety of Bodies, argues that Cause to be not blind and fortuitous, but very well skilled in Mechanicks and Geometry.

To your third Query, I answer, that it may be represented that the Sun may, by heating those Planets most which are nearest to him, cause them to be better concocted, and more condensed by that Concoction. But when I consider that our Earth is much more heated in its Bowels below the upper Crust by subterraneous Fermentations of mineral Bodies than by the Sun, I see not why the interior Parts of *Jupiter* and *Saturn* might not be as much heated, concocted, and coagulated by those Fermentations as our Earth is? and therefore this various Density should have some other Cause than the various Distances of the Planets from the Sun. And I am confirmed in this Opinion by considering, that the Planets of *Jupiter* and *Saturn*, as they are rarer than

than the reft, fo they are vaftly greater; and contain a far greater Quantity of Matter, and have many Satellites about them; which Qualifications furely arofe not from their being placed at fo great a Diftance from the Sun, but were rather the Caufe why the Creator placed them at great Diftance. For by their gravitating Powers they difturb one another's Motions very fenfibly, as I find by fome late Obfervations of Mr. *Flamfteed*, and had they been placed much nearer to the Sun and to one another, they would by the fame Powers have caufed a confiderable Difturbance in the whole Syftem.

To your fourth Query, I anfwer, that in the Hypothefis of Vortices, the Inclination of the Axis of the Earth might, in my Opinion, be afcribed to the Situation of the Earth's Vortex before it was abforbed by the neighbouring Vortices, and the Earth turned from a Sun to a

C   Comet;

Comet; but this Inclination ought to de-
creafe conftantly in Compliance with the
Motion of the Earth's Vortex, whofe
Axis is much lefs inclined to the Ecliptick, as appears by the Motion of the
Moon carried about therein. If the Sun
by his Rays could carry about the Planets, yet I do not fee how he could
thereby effect their diurnal Motions.

Laftly, I fee nothing extraordinary in
the Inclination of the Earth's Axis for
proving a Deity, unlefs you will urge it
as a Contrivance for Winter and Sum-
mer, and for making the Earth habita-
ble towards the Poles; and that the
diurnal Rotations of the Sun and Planets,
as they could hardly arife from any Caufe
purely mechanical, fo by being determined all the fame way with the annual
and menftrual Motions, they feem to
make up that Harmony in the Syftem,
which, as I explaind above, was the
Effect of Choice rather than Chance.

There

There is yet another Argument for a
Deity, which I take to be a very ftrong
one, but till the Principles on which it
is grounded are better received, I think
it more advifable to let it fleep.

I am,

Your moft humble Servant,

to command,

Cambridge,
Decemb. 10, 1692.

IS. NEWTON,

LETTER II.

For Mr. BENTLEY, *at the Palace at* Worcefter.

SIR,

I Agree with you, that if Matter evenly diffufed through a finite Space, not fpherical, fhould fall into a folid Mafs, this Mafs would affect the Figure of the whole Space, provided it were not foft, like the old Chaos, but fo hard and folid from the Beginning, that the Weight of its protuberant Parts could not make it yield to their Preffure. Yet by Earthquakes loofening the Parts of this Solid, the Protuberances might fometimes fink a little by their Weight, and thereby the Mafs might, by Degrees, approach a fpherical Figure.

The

The Reafon why Matter evenly fcat-
tered through a finite Space would convene in the midft, you conceive the fame
with me ; but that there fhould be a central Particle, fo accurately placed in the
middle, as to be always equally attracted
on all Sides, and thereby continue without Motion, feems to me a Suppofition
fully as hard as to make the fharpeft
Needle ftand upright on its Point upon a
Looking-Glafs. For if the very mathematical Center of the central Particle be
not accurately in the very mathematical
Center of the attractive Power of the
whole Mafs, the Particle will not be attracted equally on all Sides.   And much
harder it is to fuppofe all the Particles in
an infinite Space fhould be fo accurately
poifed one among another, as to ftand
ftill in a perfect Equilibrium. For I reckon
this as hard as to make not one Needle
only, but an infinite number of them (fo
many as there are Particles in an infinite
Space) ftand accurately poifed upon their
Points.

Points. Yet I grant it possible, at least by
a divine Power; and if they were once to
be placed, I agree with you that they
would continue in that Posture without
Motion for ever, unless put into new Motion by the same Power. When therefore I said, that Matter evenly spread
through all Space, would convene by its
Gravity into one or more great Masses, I
understand it of Matter not resting in an
accurate Poise.

But you argue, in the next Paragraph
of your Letter, that every Particle of
Matter in an infinite Space, has an infinite Quantity of Matter on all Sides, and
by consequence an infinite Attraction every
way, and therefore must rest in Equilibrio, because all Infinites are equal. Yet
you suspect a Paralogism in this Argument; and I conceive the Paralogism lies
in the Position, that all Infinites are equal.
The generality of Mankind consider
Infinites no other ways than indefinitely;
and

and in this Senſe, they ſay all Infinites
are equal; tho' they would ſpeak more
truly if they ſhould ſay, they are neither
equal nor unequal, nor have any certain Difference or Proportion one to another. In this Senſe therefore, no Con-
cluſions can be drawn from them, about
the Equality, Proportions, or Differences
of Things, and they that attempt to do it
uſually fall into Paralogiſms. So when
Men argue againſt the infinite Diviſibility
of Magnitude, by ſaying, that if an Inch
may be divided into an infinite Number of
Parts, the Sum of thoſe Parts will be an
Inch; and if a Foot may be divided into
an infinite Number of Parts, the Sum of
thoſe Parts muſt be a Foot, and therefore
ſince all Infinites are equal, thoſe Sums
muſt be equal, that is, an Inch equal to
a Foot.

The Falſeneſs of the Concluſion ſhews
an Error in the Premiſes, and the Error
lies in the Poſition, that all Infinites are
equal.

equal. There is therefore another Way of confidering Infinites ufed by Mathematicians, and that is, under certain definite Reftrictions and Limitations, whereby Infinites are determined to have certain Differences or Proportions to one another. Thus Dr. *Wallis* confiders them in his *Arithmetica Infinitorum*, where by the various Proportions of infinite Sums, he gathers the various Proportions of infinite Magnitudes: Which way of arguing is generally allowed by Mathematicians, and yet would not be good were all Infinites equal. According to the fame way of confidering Infinites, a Mathematician would tell you, that tho' there be an infinite Number of infinite little Parts in an Inch, yet there is twelve times that Number of fuch Parts in a Foot, that is, the infinite Number of thofe Parts in a Foot is not equal to, but twelve Times bigger than the infinite Number of them in an Inch. And fo a Mathematician will tell you, that if a

D   Body

Body ftood in Equilibrio between any two equal and contrary attracting infinite Forces; and if to either of thefe Forces you add any new finite attracting Force, that new Force, how little foever, will deftroy their Equilibrium, and put the Body into the fame Motion into which it would put it were thofe two contrary equal Forces but finite, or even none at all; fo that in this Cafe the two equal Infinites by the Addition of a Finite to either of them, become unequal in our ways of Reckoning; and after thefe ways we muft reckon, if from the Confiderations of Infinites we would always draw true Conclufions.

To the laft Part of your Letter, I anfwer, Firft, that if the Earth (without the Moon) were placed any where with its Center in the *Orbis Magnus*, and ftood ftill there without any Gravitation or Projection, and there at once were infufed into it, both a gravitating Energy towards the

the Sun, and a tranſverſe Impulſe of a juſt Quantity moving it directly in a Tangent to the *Orbis Magnus*; the Compounds of this Attraction and Projection would, according to my Notion, cauſe a circular Revolution of the Earth about the Sun. But the tranſverſe Impulſe muſt be a juſt Quantity; for if it be too big or too little, it will cauſe the Earth to move in ſome other Line. Secondly, I do not know any Power in Nature which would cauſe this tranſverſe Motion without the divine Arm. *Blondel* tells us ſomewhere in his Book of Bombs, that *Plato* affirms, that the Motion of the Planets is ſuch, as if they had all of them been created by God in ſome Region very remote from our Syſtem, and let fall from thence towards the Sun, and ſo ſoon as they arrived at their ſeveral Orbs, their Motion of falling turned aſide into a tranſverſe one. And this is true, ſuppoſing the gravitating Power of the Sun was double

at

at that Moment of Time in which they
all arrive at their feveral Orbs ; but then
the divine Power is here required in a
double refpect, namely, to turn the defcending Motions of the falling Planets
into a fide Motion, and at the fame time
to double the attractive Power of the Sun.
So then Gravity may put the Planets into
Motion, but without the divine Power it
could never put them into fuch a circulating
Motion as they have about the Sun ; and
therefore, for this, as well as other Reafons,
I am compelled to afcribe the Frame of
this Syftem to an intelligent Agent.

You fometimes fpeak of Gravity as
effential and inherent to Matter. Pray do
not afcribe that Notion to me ; for the
Caufe of Gravity is what I do not pretend
to know, and therefore would take more
Time to confider of it.

I fear what I have faid of Infinites, will
feem obfcure to you ; but it is enough if
you

you underftand, that Infinites when confidered abfolutely without any Reftriction
or Limitation, are neither equal nor unequal, nor have any certain Proportion one
to another, and therefore the Principle
that all Infinites are equal, is a precarious
one.

Sir, I am,

    Your moft humble Servant,

Trinity College,
Jan. 17, 1692-3.

IS. NEWTON.

L E T-

LETTER III.

For Mr. BENTLEY, *at the Palace at* Worcester.

SIR,

BEcause you desire Speed, I will answer your Letter with what Brevity I can. In the six Positions you lay down in the Beginning of your Letter, I agree with you. Your assuming the *Orbis Magnus* 7000 Diameters of the Earth wide, implies the Sun's horizontal Parallax to be half a Minute. *Flamsteed* and *Cassini* have of late observed it to be about 10″, and thus the *Orbis Magnus* must be 21,000, or in a rounder Number 20,000 Diameters of the Earth wide. Either Computation I

think

think will do well, and I think it not worth while to alter your Numbers.

In the next Part of your Letter you lay down four other Pofitions, founded upon the fix firft. The firft of thefe four feems very evident, fuppofing you take Attraction fo generally as by it to underftand any Force by which diftant Bodies endeavour to come together without mechanical Impulfe. The fecond feems not fo clear ; for it may be faid, that there might be other Syftems of Worlds before the prefent ones, and others before thofe, and fo on to all paft Eternity, and by confequence, that Gravity may be co-eternal to Matter, and have the fame Effect from all Eternity as at prefent, unlefs you have fomewhere proved that old Syftems cannot gradually pafs into new ones ; or that this Syftem had not its Original from the exhaling Matter of former decaying Syftems, but from a Chaos of Matter evenly
difperfed

difperfed throughout all Space ; for fomething of this Kind, I think, you fay was
the Subject of your fixth Sermon ; and
the Growth of new Syftems out of old
ones, without the Mediation of a divine
Power, feems to me apparently abfurd,

The laft Claufe of the fecond Pofition
I like very well. It is inconceivable, that
inanimate brute Matter fhould, without
the Mediation of fomething elfe, which is
not material, operate upon, and affect
other Matter without mutual Contact, as
it muft be, if Gravitation in the Senfe of
Epicurus, be effential and inherent in it.
And this is one Reafon why I defired you
would not afcribe innate Gravity to me.
That Gravity fhould be innate, inherent
and effential to Matter, fo that one Body
may act upon another at a Diftance thro'
a *Vacuum,* without the Mediation of any
thing elfe, by and through which their
Action and Force may be conveyed from

E   one

one to another, is to me so great an Absurdity, that I believe no Man who has in philosophical Matters a competent Faculty of thinking, can ever fall into it. Gravity must be caused by an Agent acting constantly according to certain Laws; but whether this Agent be material or immaterial, I have left to the Consideration of my Readers,

Your fourth Affertion, that the World could not be formed by innate Gravity alone, you confirm by three Arguments. But in your first Argument you feem to make a *Petitio Principii*; for whereas many ancient Philofophers and others, as well Theifts as Atheifts, have all allowed, that there may be Worlds and Parcels of Matter innumerable or infinite, you deny this, by reprefenting it as abfurd as that there fhould be pofitively an infinite arithmetical Sum or Number, which is a Contradiction *in Terminis*; but you do not

prove

prove it as abſurd. Neither do you prove, that what Men mean by an infinite Sum or Number, is a Contradiction in Nature; for a Contradiction *in Terminis* implies no more than an Impropriety of Speech. Thoſe things which Men underſtand by improper and contradictious Phraſes, may be ſometimes really in Nature without any Contradiction at all: a Silver Inkhorn, a Paper Lanthorn, an Iron Whetſtone, are abſurd Phraſes, yet the Things ſignified thereby, are really in Nature. If any Man ſhould ſay, that a Number and a Sum, to ſpeak properly, is that which may be numbered and ſummed, but Things infinite are numberleſs, or, as we uſually ſpeak, innumerable and ſumleſs, or inſummable, and therefore ought not to be called a Number or Sum, he will ſpeak properly enough, and your Argument againſt him will, I fear, loſe its Force. And yet if any Man ſhall take the Words, Number and Sum, in a larger Senſe, ſo

as

as to underſtand thereby Things, which
in the proper way of ſpeaking are numberleſs and ſumleſs (as you ſeem to do
when you allow an infinite Number of
Points in a Line) I could readily allow him
the Uſe of the contradictious Phraſes of
innumerable Number, or ſumleſs Sum,
without inferring from thence any Abſur-
dity in the Thing he means by thoſe
Phraſes. However, if by this, or any
other Argument, you have proved the
Finiteneſs of the Univerſe; it follows, that
all Matter would fall down from the Out-
ſides, and convene in the Middle. Yet
the Matter in falling might concrete into
many round Maſſes, like the Bodies of
the Planets, and theſe by attracting one
another, might acquire an Obliquity of
Deſcent, by means of which they might
fall, not upon the great central Body, but
upon the Side of it, and fetch a Compaſs
about, and then aſcend again by the ſame
Steps and Degrees of Motion and Velocity
with

with which they defcended before, much
after the Manner that the Comets revolve
about the Sun; but a circular Motion in
concentrick Orbs about the Sun, they
could never acquire by Gravity alone.

And tho' all the Matter were divided at
firft into feveral Syftems, and every Syftem by a divine Power conftituted like
ours; yet would the Outfide Syftems defcend towards the Middlemoft; fo that
this Frame of Things could not always
fubfift without a divine Power to conferve
it, which is the fecond Argument; and
to your third I fully affent.

As for the Paffage of *Plato*, there is no
common Place from whence all the Planets being let fall, and defcending with
uniform and equal Gravities (as *Galileo*
fuppofes) would at their Arrival to their
feveral Orbs acquire their feveral Velocities, with which they now revolve in
them.

them. If we fuppofe the Gravity of all the Planets towards the Sun to be of fuch à Quantity as it really is, and that the Motions of the Planets are turned upwards, every Planet will afcend to twice its Height from the Sun. *Saturn* will afcend till he be twice as high from the Sun as he is at prefent, and no higher; *Jupiter* will afcend as high again as at prefent, that is, a little above the Orb of *Saturn*; *Mercury* will afcend to twice his prefent Height, that is, to the Orb of *Venus*; and fo of the reft; and then by falling down again from the Places to which they afcended, they will arrive again at their feveral Orbs with the fame Velocities they had at firft, and with which they now revolve.

But if fo foon as their Motions by which they revolve are turned upwards, the gravitating Power of the Sun, by which their Afcent is perpetually retarded,

be

be diminished by one half, they will now ascend perpetually, and all of them at all equal Distances from the Sun will be equally swift. *Mercury* when he arrives at the Orb of *Venus*, will be as swift as *Venus*; and he and *Venus*, when they arrive at the Orb of the *Earth*, will be as swift as the *Earth*; and so of the rest. If they begin all of them to ascend at once, and ascend in the same Line, they will constantly in ascending become nearer and nearer together, and their Motions will constantly approach to an Equality, and become at length slower than any Motion assignable. Suppose therefore, that they ascended till they were almost contiguous, and their Motions inconsiderably little, and that all their Motions were at the same Moment of Time turned back again; or, which comes almost to the same Thing, that they were only deprived of their Motions, and let fall at that Time, they would all at once arrive at their several Orbs, each

with

with the Velocity it had at firft; and if their Motions were then turned Sideways, and at the fame Time the gravitating Power of the Sun doubled, that it might be ftrong enough to retain them in their Orbs, they would revolve in them as before their Afcent. But if the gravitateing Power of the Sun was not doubled, they would go away from their Orbs into the higheft Heavens in parabolical Lines. Thefe Things follow from my *Princ. Math. Lib.* i. *Prop.* 33, 34, 36, 37.

I thank you very kindly for your defigned Prefent, and reft

Your moft

humble Servant

to command,

Cambridge,
Feb. 25, 1692-3.

IS. NEWTON.

LETTER IV.

To Mr. BENTLEY, *at the Palace at* Worcefter.

S I R,

THE Hypothefis of deriving the Frame of the World by mechanical Principles from Matter evenly fpread through the Heavens, being inconfiftent with my Syftem, I had confidered it very little before your Letters put me upon it, and therefore trouble you with a Line or two more about it, if this comes not too late for your Ufe.

In my former I reprefented that the diurnal Rotations of the Planets could not be derived from Gravity, but required a divine Arm to imprefs them. And tho'

F   Gravity

Gravity might give the Planets a Motion of Defcent towards the Sun, either directly or with fome little Obliquity, yet the tranfverfe Motions by which they revolve in their feveral Orbs, required the divine Arm to imprefs them according to the Tangents of their Orbs. I would now add, that the Hypothefis of Matter's being at firft evenly fpread through the Heavens, is, in my Opinion, inconfiftent with the Hypothefis of innate Gravity, without a fupernatural Power to reconcile them, and therefore it infers a Deity. For if there be innate Gravity, it is impoffible now for the Matter of the Earth and all the Planets and Stars to fly up from them, and become evenly fpread throughout all the Heavens, without a fupernatural Power; and certainly that which can never be hereafter without a fupernatural Power, could never be heretofore without the fame Power.

You

You queried, whether Matter evenly spread throughout a finite Space, of some other Figure than spherical, would not in falling down towards a central Body, cause that Body to be of the same Figure with the whole Space, and I answered, yes. But in my Answer it is to be supposed that the Matter descends directly downwards to that Body, and that that Body has no diurnal Rotation.

This, Sir, is all I would add to **my** former Letters.

I am,

Your most humble

Servant,

Cambridge,
Feb. 11, 1693.

IS. NEWTON.

F I N I S.

CPSIA information can be obtained
at www.ICGtesting.com
Printed in the USA
BVHW060413221221
624643BV00002B/30